WHO TO T

This book lays out what it means t
Christian life runs counter to many
eternal rewards are stupendous. It'
fence!

Copyright 2014 Graham Charles Cumming

Published by Graham Cumming

All the Bible references are quoted from the 1965 Bible in Basic English

Updates on my books are available on these links:

www.beginningwithadam.blogspot.com.au

www.authorsden.com/grahamccumming

www.jacketflap.com/gracum

TABLE OF CONTENTS

Pointers To God
Making Your Choice
Right And Wrong
Life

POINTERS TO GOD

A store sign blatantly announced:

In God we Trust.

Everybody else pays Cash!

The media is full of stories of people duped into parting with their savings for schemes that are scams. Knowing who will be honest and reliable with your resources is a real issue in these days. A more crucial decision is who to trust with your life! With so many choices clamouring for your attention, how do you make up your mind? Some scientists and philosophers are proponents of atheism. Others are convinced of the existence of a god or gods. Many people by default fall into the middle category of agnosticism, admitting they do not know. You may be in that position. If so, this book is for you.

If you are already convinced that God is out there somewhere, but you have made a mess of your life up to this point, you may be worried that he is angry with you. You could be worried that you are beyond forgiveness, and that your eternal destiny will be hell rather than heaven. Keep reading, because there is a God, who made you and loves you, in spite of whatever you may have done to upset him. Nobody is too wicked to find peace and restoration, because he has paid the costly price to redeem imperfect men, women and children.

All of humanity is aware of a spiritual vacuum – an empty space only God can fill. We are searching for supernatural answers. Our conscience is alive and kicking. Deep down we know there is more to life than what we can experience with our physical senses. Strong emotions like the pity we feel for the starving or the sacrificial love parents have for their children remind us that we are more than flesh and blood. Both our tears of grief and our sense of humour reinforce the idea that man is far superior to the animals. This is because God has built his own nature into the human heart:

> *And God made man in his image, in the image of God he made him: male and female he made them.*
>
> *(Genesis 1:27)*

This verse in the Bible says it twice to underline the point. Down through history mankind has possessed sensitivity to the supernatural. This characteristic which differentiates us so significantly from animals manifests itself in a variety of ways. That man has a need to worship something or someone superior is demonstrated by the plethora of world religions. Also the existence of witchcraft, wizardry, sorcery and similar dark practices remind us that there is a corresponding evil force. The on-going hidden battle between the opposing kingdoms of light and darkness, good and evil, truth and falsehood is unwittingly acknowledged when people say, 'Fingers crossed,' 'Touch wood' and other superstitious phrases. Having entered the third millennium should we ditch the supernatural as a relic of the past or is there a continuing spiritual reality?

Faith

Nobody will ever offer conclusive proof that everything was created by God. Ultimately it comes down to a position of faith. I used to go along with the majority view that life evolved, but after becoming a Christian I just knew I'd been deceived. The Theory of Evolution is still unproven, even though the majority of scientists and academics believe it to be true. Their faith is unfounded, based on presupposition and prejudice. If you want to know how deceptive evolution is, you may like to read my book, 'How We Began.'

Through the eyes of faith in Jesus Christ, the Son of God, I began to see everything in a new light, and from this fresh perspective, I embarked on a quest for the truth. As the writer of Hebrews says:

Now faith is the substance of things hoped for, and the sign that the things not seen are true.

For by it our fathers had God's approval.

By faith it is clear to us that the order of events was fixed by the word of God, so that what is seen has not been made from things which only seem to be.

And without faith it is not possible to be well-pleasing to him, for it is necessary for anyone who comes to God to have the belief that God is, and that he is a rewarder of all those who make a serious search for him.

By faith Noah, being moved by the fear of God, made ready an ark for the salvation of his family, because God had given him news of things which were not seen at the time; and through it the world was judged by him, and he got for his heritage the righteousness which is by faith.

(Hebrews 11:1-3 & 6-7).

Does God Exist?

An atheist colleague of mine was deeply entrenched in evolution as the explanation of life. He used to argue that if God was there, he ought to show himself or communicate audibly. In the absence of such evidence he concluded God was simply a figment of the human imagination. Many humanists reason that unless God gives them a concrete sign they will not believe he exists. This appears logical until you start to delve deeper. In using this line of argument humanists are puffing up their own importance and reducing God to their own size. If God created everything from the tiniest atom to the vast Universe, he must be amazingly big, fantastically clever, supremely authoritative and infinitely awesome. Why would such an immense God take any notice of a whinging little person saying, 'Give me a sign or I won't believe in you'? God reserves the right to hide himself! Actually, though, there are a number of signposts pointing towards him.

Signpost 1

The obvious one is the orderliness, intricacy and beauty of everything around us.

> *For from the first making of the world, those things of God which the eye is unable to see, that is, his eternal power and existence, are fully made clear, he having given the knowledge of them through the things which he has made, so that men have no reason for wrongdoing:*
>
> (Romans 1:20)

Some fail to see this sign, because their belief in evolution automatically rules God out of the picture. Consequently God conceals himself:

> *And for this cause, God will give them up to the power of deceit and they will put their faith in what is false:*
>
> (2 Thessalonians 2:11)

There are so many everyday things we rely on and take for granted. Suppose when you tap a snooker ball with a cue that you have no control over the direction in which it will travel. The game would produce haphazard results with no advantage derived from the acquisition of skills. It would be pointlessly boring! Our weather forecasters are able to predict temperatures, sunshine and rainfall with dependable accuracy six or seven days ahead, but what if climate patterns were completely random? No one would know from one minute to the next if it was going to rain, hail or shine. Anything could happen, so it would be almost impossible to venture outdoors, not knowing whether to expect a burning heat wave, an icy blizzard or a drenching downpour.

Think for a moment about numbers. Computation would have been extremely difficult in Roman times. Even with the help of an abacus sums like CLXXIV + MCCXLVII must have severely taxed the brains of young Roman scholars, and subtraction, multiplication and division would have been substantially harder.

The Romans built great roads, but mathematics did not really take off until we hit on Arabic numerals, which, according to the *Oxford Reference Dictionary*, possibly originated in India and reached Western Europe around 1200 AD. With decimal notation the simplicity, orderliness and amazing beauty of numbers became apparent.

$$1 \times 8 + 1 = 9$$
$$12 \times 8 + 2 = 98$$
$$123 \times 8 + 3 = 987$$
$$1234 \times 8 + 4 = 9876$$
$$12345 \times 8 + 5 = 98765$$
$$123456 \times 8 + 6 = 987654$$
$$1234567 \times 8 + 7 = 9876543$$
$$12345678 \times 8 + 8 = 98765432$$
$$123456789 \times 8 + 9 = 987654321$$

$$1 \times 9 + 2 = 11$$
$$12 \times 9 + 3 = 111$$
$$123 \times 9 + 4 = 1111$$
$$1234 \times 9 + 5 = 11111$$
$$12345 \times 9 + 6 = 111111$$
$$123456 \times 9 + 7 = 1111111$$
$$1234567 \times 9 + 8 = 11111111$$
$$12345678 \times 9 + 9 = 111111111$$
$$123456789 \times 9 + 10 = 1111111111$$

$$1 \times 1 = 1$$
$$11 \times 11 = 121$$
$$111 \times 111 = 12321$$
$$1111 \times 1111 = 1234321$$
$$11111 \times 11111 = 123454321$$
$$111111 \times 111111 = 12345654321$$
$$1111111 \times 1111111 = 1234567654321$$
$$11111111 \times 11111111 = 123456787654321$$
$$111111111 \times 111111111 = 12345678987654321$$

Fascinating geometrical shapes and numerical patterns recurring in nature have been discovered by people like Leonardo Fibonacci, born in 1175 and Benoit Mandelbrot, who died aged 85 in 2010. *Fibonacci Numbers* still figure in the educational curriculum today, and the animated *Mandelbrot Fractals* are so inspiringly colourful they have a cult following on the internet. There is a whole world of mathematical complexity and beauty still under exploration by great thinkers of our time.

The same is true of music. The realisation that there is an underlying arrangement of tones and semi-tones, sharps and flats in a recurring pattern of octaves prepared the way for all the great composers of recent centuries. Similarly the inventors of radio, television, telephony, photography, cinematography, flight, computers and a host of other wonders all depended on the existence of specific scientific rules or modes of behaviour already in existence. Their discoveries simply built on established natural laws waiting to be harnessed and used. Those we observe in operation point to a Lawgiver.

Aborigines discovered numerous natural remedies including aromatic herbs, tannin-rich inner barks, roots, witchetty grubs, crushed termite mounds, honey ants, melaleuca and eucalyptus, which is still widely used in lozenges and other preparations to relieve blocked noses. Healing medicines have been found to exist for most diseases, and the search continues for others. Pharmaceutical companies are engaged in endless research exploring the natural world for undiscovered substances and performing clinical trials to test their efficacy. Fortunately the majority of hurts we experience in the normal course of life heal naturally without a great deal of effort. Bruises gradually fade as the burst capillaries mend themselves and lose their soreness. Minor cuts and grazes heal over and the skin becomes as good as new, if kept clean. Even broken bones will grow back together when supported by a splint or cast. The way our body mends itself and the amazing availability of cures for most diseases suggests that our Maker is also in the business of being our Healer.

Consider the array of colours and the range of calls of our birds. The way in which they build their nests, lay their eggs and hatch and nurture their young is so amazing. The phenomenon of sexual reproduction in animals and especially in man is such a miraculous gift. Surely no father who has witnessed the birth of his first child can deny the beauty of this arrangement. Take a few moments to consider the numerous ways in which plants and trees spread their seeds. Some like the dandelion and sycamore are blown by the wind. Some have barbs which cling to animal fur and human clothing. Some are distributed by birds, some harvested and planted by man and there are many more ingenious methods.

Look at our varieties of felines, canines, marsupials, reptiles and insects. Explore the underwater beauty of the Great Barrier Reef, one of the world's most complex ecosystems with 400 species of corals, 4000 species of molluscs and 1500 species of fish. Then recognise that our planet is merely one sphere among millions in the solar system and countless remote galaxies. In total contrast zoom right in and focus on the tiniest specks of cellular life in the human body. Even these minute organisms have a design and complexity too clever for man to replicate. The infinite vastness of space and the microscopic complexity of chromosomes, genes and DNA indicate the existence of a powerful creative force with no top or bottom limits. The intricacy, richness and beauty of nature surely could not exist without a benevolent Provider. The existence of colour from black to white with all the infinite hues in between is a miracle in itself, and so is our ability to see every shape and shade three-dimensionally! Planning is so evident in the natural world that we have ample reason to expect there to have been a Designer with unlimited imagination and creativity.

God doesn't push in where he is not wanted! He is light and light never forces itself through a closed door! God hides himself from those who deny or ignore him, but reveals himself to all who open the door and invite him in:

> *Come near to God and he will come near to you. Make your hands clean, you evil-doers; put away deceit from your hearts, you false in mind.*
>
> *(James 4:8)*

Signpost 2

> *Researchers at the University of Oxford will spend £1.9 million investigating why people believe in God. Academics have been given a grant to try to find out whether belief in a deity is a matter of nature or nurture. [Ruth Gledhill, Religion Correspondent; The Times, February 19, 2008.]*

It would be reasonable to expect that if God exists, he would express himself to enable us to know him. He has. The second signpost is the Bible. This amazing collection of writings is unlike any other 'holy' book. It is available in nearly every known language and is the world's bestseller. It is widely quoted, frequently criticized, often ridiculed, but seldom read in its entirety. It has stood the test of time, having been completed nearly two thousand years ago. It has survived many attempts to eradicate it. The Bible consists of 66 books penned by around 40 different writers through a period of 2000 years, yet it is authoritative and supernaturally consistent. The content is powerfully motivational and purports to be the inspired word of God:

> *Every holy Writing which comes from God is of profit for teaching, for training, for guiding, for education in righteousness:*
>
> *(2 Timothy 3:16)*

In other words he expressed himself through carefully selected human scribes. This is a tremendous claim, and the only way to verify it is to read it right through for yourself. Unlike any other sacred writing the Bible is self-authenticating as you read its pages and experience the Creator of the universe talking directly to you. Don't struggle with a Bible in archaic language, but use a modern translation such as the New International Version or New King James. Try reading the New Testament section first, starting with the four Gospels and 'Acts of the Apostles' before progressing to the Old Testament. A number of Bible-reading helps are available from publishers such as *Scripture Union*.

Signpost 3

As you continue through the Bible you will come face to face with the clearest signpost of all. If you want to know exactly what God is like, look at his Son. Jesus referred to God as his 'Father.' His human mother was Mary. She had a number of sons and daughters, but her husband Joseph did not father the first one. Mary was a virgin until God placed his own Son in her womb. Jesus was both Son of God and Son of Man. He was fully divine and completely human. Everything he said and did reflected the character of God. He was the one and only perfect human being ever to have lived. Because God was his Father his human nature was totally unblemished:

> *For we have not a high priest who is not able to be touched by the feelings of our feeble flesh; but we have one who has been tested in all points as we ourselves are tested, but without sin.*

> *(Hebrews 4:15)*

Jesus came on a rescue mission. His name means 'Saviour.' The nature of all mankind is tainted and warped. We lost the perfection with which we were created and can never regain it by our own efforts. The disobedience of our ancestors has been passed on from parent to child down through the centuries:

> *For this reason, as through one man sin came into the world, and death because of sin, and so death came to all men, because all have done evil:*
>
> *(Romans 5:12)*
>
> *Truly, I was formed in evil, and in sin did my mother give me birth.*
>
> *(Psalm 51:5)*

You received your fallen, imperfect human nature from your parents, and you will pass it on to your children. Unless somehow your perfection can be restored, you are cut off from God's presence. He is holy and cannot tolerate evil anywhere near him. If you die in your imperfection, you are doomed to an eternal separation from God. The Bible calls this Hell:

> *Whose reward will be eternal destruction from the face of the Lord and from the glory of his strength,*
>
> *At his coming, when he will have glory in his saints, and will be a cause of wonder in all those who had faith because our witness among you had effect in that day.*
>
> *(2 Thessalonians 1:9-10)*

Heaven is being with God forever. Jesus came to rescue you from Hell and open up the way into Heaven. Because of God's holiness he decreed that the penalty for your imperfection is death, both physical and spiritual. However, God also loves you deeply and has provided a way of saving you from this condemnation. Another perfect human being had to be willing to die instead of you. Jesus, God's son, voluntarily gave his life in your place. He paid your penalty by offering his life as a sacrifice so that you can go free. Jesus said he was sacrificing himself for the sake of those who follow him:

> *Even as the Father has knowledge of me and I of the Father; and I am giving my life for the sheep.*
>
> *(John 10:15)*

You are totally forgiven, your peace with God is restored and the way to Heaven is open before you. All you have to do to receive it is believe it. We have been made right with God by putting our trust in what Jesus Christ has done:

> *For which reason, because we have righteousness through faith, let us be at peace with God through our Lord Jesus Christ;*
>
> *(Romans 5:1).*

Jesus suffered crucifixion – probably the most agonizing death invented by man. It occurred significantly on the day of 'Preparation' for the Jewish festival of 'Passover' – the very day that the sacrificial lambs were slaughtered. He died and was laid in a tomb, but he didn't stay dead! Early on the following Sunday morning he rose from death to life. He showed himself to his followers, who were amazed. His new resurrected body was solid and could eat and drink, yet it could pass through locked doors, move instantly from one place to another, appear, disappear and rise in the air. One day he will return and then we too will have an immortal body like his:

> *My loved ones, now we are children of God, and at present it is not clear what we are to be. We are certain that at his revelation we will be like him; for we will see him as he is.*
>
> *(1 John 3:2)*
>
> *See, I am giving you the revelation of a secret: we will not all come to the sleep of death, but we will all be changed.*
>
> *In a second, in the shutting of an eye, at the sound of the last horn: for at that sound the dead will come again, free for ever from the power of death, and we will be changed.*

(1 Corinthians 15:51-52)

Ian McCormack from New Zealand received multiple jellyfish stings while scuba diving. Although his Christian mother had been regularly praying for him, he had been an atheist, living his life in a completely self-centred kind of style. As he lay dying he made his peace with God and received full forgiveness and acceptance. He was rushed to hospital but died as the poison progressively shut down his vital organs. Fifteen minutes later as he was being prepared to go on the slab in the mortuary he came to life again, and made a full recovery – totally healed. He describes vividly and emotionally his out of body experience while clinically dead.

He first experienced Hell – a region of utter darkness and isolation, but was drawn to a narrow shaft of intense light. As he moved up through this increasing brightness he felt enveloped in love, joy and peace. He witnessed the indescribable beauty of Heaven, encountered God and was given the choice to stay or return. Out of love and concern for his mother he decided to return, and he has been freely recounting his amazing story to thousands of enthralled listeners ever since. Further details are available on his website. [http://www.aglimpseofeternity.org] Someone asked:

> *Why do you think God chose to intervene in the case of Ian McCormack when he has failed to do so in far more 'deserving and tragic' incidents?*

This is a sincere and deep question, deserving an answer. Ian McCormack travels round the world telling his story. He came to our church in Canberra a few years ago and spoke it out with a mix of humour, sincerity and emotion. I have no doubt as to the reality of his experience, incredible as it sounds. Why did God intervene in his case? – because he had a specific mission in mind for Ian and knew he would accomplish it. Why doesn't God always respond in this way? If he always immediately corrected every tragedy, it would remove a large element of human responsibility. It would also counteract or diminish the effects resulting from the exercise of man's free will to do good or to do evil. God gave us free will because he desires a genuine, unforced love from us. God can, and occasionally does, overrule natural laws, but if he always interfered with expected outcomes, they would no longer be laws.

The response God most wants from us is faith in himself. If he always intervened in every case, deserving or otherwise, there would be no need for faith. Who decides whether one case is more deserving or more tragic than another? There are so many hidden, unknown factors that only God is capable of making that kind of decision with accuracy and justice. If God doesn't intervene, it's because he chooses not to. Humans may fail, but God never does. We think and operate under human time limits. God has eternity and infinite resources. Think of Jesus' parable of the rich man and Lazarus. Any injustices, tragedies or disasters will be put right in the next life. Likewise, any unsolved, unpunished or unforgiven crimes in this age will be dealt with in eternity.

<><><><><>

Updates on my books are available on these links:

www.beginningwithadam.blogspot.com.au

www.authorsden.com/grahamccumming

www.jacketflap.com/gracum

<><><><><>

MAKING YOUR CHOICE

There are times in our life when we become more acutely aware of our need for God's presence. In times of extreme danger or anguish even the toughest cry out for his help. You may be travelling through a dark wilderness right now. Perhaps you have been physically or mentally abused. Someone you love deeply may be suffering or may have died. You may be burdened with serious financial stress. Mistakes you have made may have left you in painful turmoil. You may feel that your whole life is upside down.

While passing through such times of distress many people testify that in their extremity they sensed God's presence most tangibly. He responded to their crisis with mercy, love, compassion and emotional healing. As they reached out to him they discovered he is as solid and dependable as a rock, a comforting light in their darkness and a rich source of hope and guidance. Certainly there was a defining moment for me when I allowed God to come in and sort out the mess I had made of my life. Sometimes it's as if God takes his hands off and leaves us to get into a pickle just to get our attention!

You may think you control the direction of your life. In reality, though, no-one can determine the course of even one day. Too many factors come into play. Ultimately – like it or not – God is in the driving seat:

> *How foolish it is to say, Today or tomorrow we will go into this town, and be there for a year and do business there and get wealth:*
>
> *(James 4:13)*

Vacate the driving position, and let God have the wheel. He knows what is best for you and can be trusted implicitly to steer you in the right direction. Whenever you push him out and take over the controls you can be sure that you will end up in the wrong place.

It's really a question of priorities. Which is more important - your present temporary life or eternity? The issue is black and white. Either live for yourself and your own worldly pleasures, or put what God wants at the top of your list:

> *No man is able to be a servant to two masters: for he will have hate for the one and love for the other, or he will keep to one and have no respect for the other. You may not be servants of God and of wealth.*
>
> (Matthew 6:24)

Money is a useful tool, but an all-consuming boss. Remember that your wealth and material possessions are all on loan to you from God, and he can remove all of it in a few seconds, if he chooses. Acknowledge this by handing over the control of your finance and all you own to him. When you do this he will make sure that you have all you really need:

> *But let your first care be for his kingdom and his righteousness; and all these other things will be given to you in addition.*
>
> (Matthew 6:33)

Who or what is at the top of your list? God promises to clothe you, feed you and take care of all your requirements, if you put him first. Remember also that God wants you to be well in body, soul and spirit. Jesus showed that God cares about your body as well as your spirit when he demonstrated the love and power of God in many miraculous healings. He still heals today. Ask God for healing. He has the power and he wants you to be whole in every way.

Commitment

There is nothing worse than living from day to day with no motivation – like the sad person who admitted, 'I used to be indecisive, but now I'm not so sure.' If your life is without purpose, there is only one direction you will take and that is downwards. Robert Louis Stevenson's bizarre tale of 'The Strange Case of Dr Jekyll and Mr Hyde' graphically spells out the dangers of trying to live in two opposite worlds. Sitting on the fence is not an option. You need to make your choice. Jesus said,

> *Whoever is not with me is against me; and he who does not take part with me in getting people together, is driving them away.*
>
> *(Matthew 12:30)*

It's time to stop trying to sit on the fence and decide whether you believe life began on its own 4,600 million years ago or whether God created life a mere 6,000 or so years ago.

Evolution's implied optimistic outlook on life belies its reality. Its doctrine of continuous improvement contrasts disappointingly with its moral bankruptcy. Its product is an empty materialism. It offers post-modern man a foundation of sand on which to build his life. If we simply evolved by chance, we are masters of our own destiny. We can do what we want. There is no right or wrong. If it feels good, do it. Life is the survival of the fittest. There is no life after death, so we shall not be called to account for our actions, and therefore we are free to satisfy our basic desires. It makes no difference whether you are heterosexual, bisexual or homosexual. Promiscuity is fine. Marriage is outmoded. Abortion is no big deal. Alcohol, drugs, gluttony and pornography are there to be enjoyed. Everything is relative, so theft, lying, adultery and even murder can be justified. Guilt is just a feeling to be ignored.

At the same time we hear news of earthquakes, tsunamis, landslides, volcanic eruptions, wars, nuclear bombs, terrorist atrocities, global warming, drought, famine, thinning of the ozone layer and the acceleration of modern plagues like AIDS, Bird Flu and Swine Flu. A host of disasters graphically persuade us that things in general are going downhill fast! This all strikes us as being far removed from the theme of 'continuous improvement.'

The contrast is so inexplicable that we may either have to ignore it or risk schizophrenia!

There is no middle ground. Abstention is a 'No' vote. If you do not stand up for Jesus, you are letting him down and propagating the cause of his evil enemy, Satan. Be on fire for God, because he is passionate for zeal and enthusiasm:

> *I have knowledge of your works, that you are not cold or warm: it would be better if you were cold or warm.*
>
> *So because you are not one thing or the other, I will have no more to do with you.*
>
> *(Revelation 3:15-16)*

Nominal Christians make God sick! Either get on board or jump off. If you still have nagging doubts, talk them through with a Christian you trust. James had this to say about the person who cannot make up his mind:

> *Let him make his request in faith, doubting nothing; for he who has doubt in his heart is like the waves of the sea, which are troubled by the driving of the wind.*
>
> *Let it not seem to such a man that he will get anything from the Lord;*
>
> *For there is a division in his mind, and he is uncertain in all his ways.*
>
> *(James 1:6-8)*

Understand not only that God exists, but that he exercises ultimate power and authority over you and every living being. He is to be revered and given the 'Number One' slot in all your decision-making. If there is anything you are unsure about, anything you need advice on, listen to the recommendation of wise King Solomon:

> *The fear of the Lord is the start of wisdom, and the knowledge of the Holy One gives a wise mind*
>
> *(Proverbs 9:10)*

The starting point for becoming wise (not clever, intelligent or brainy) is bowing down before the awesome greatness of God. Certain highly privileged characters in the Bible were allowed to approach into his near presence and these tough, faithful people were totally overawed by the experience. It shook them to the core. One of these was the great prophet Elijah, who asked the people of Israel:

> *And Elijah came near to all the people and said, How long will you go on balancing between two opinions? if the Lord is God, then give worship to him; but if Baal, give worship to him. And the people said not a word in answer.*
>
> *(1 Kings 18:21)*

They responded with a renewed commitment to end worship of the false god Baal, and threw in their wholehearted support for the one true God, whom they referred to as 'Yahweh' or 'Jehovah.' Like ourselves the Israelites needed continual reminders to sort out their priorities. On another occasion following the death of Moses they were challenged by their new leader Joshua:

> *And if it seems evil to you to be the servants of the Lord, make the decision this day whose servants you will be: of the gods whose servants your fathers were across the River, or of the gods of the Amorites in whose land you are living: but I and my house will be the servants of the Lord.*
>
> *(Joshua 24:15)*

Simple Faith

There is nothing complicated about becoming a follower of Jesus Christ. It is open to male and female of every race, every level of intelligence, every social class and every background. He said you will not enter the Kingdom of God unless you have childlike trust:

> *Truly I say to you, Whoever does not put himself under the*

> kingdom of God like a little child, will not come into it at all.
>
> (Luke 18:17)

Trying to be too clever can be a hindrance. By choosing the foolish God has embarrassed those who consider themselves wise. God welcomes simple faith:

> But God made selection of the foolish things of this world so that he might put the wise to shame; and the feeble things that he might put to shame the strong;
>
> (1 Corinthians 1:27)

Wealth also may be a barrier. Entering the Kingdom involves surrendering yourself and everything you possess to God. Jesus graphically described how hard it is for a rich person to get into the Kingdom:

> And again I say to you, It is simpler for a camel to go through a needle's eye, than for a man with much money to go into the kingdom of God.
>
> (Matthew 19:24)

To become a Christian demands total trust and commitment. Following Christ means denying yourself and being prepared to suffer for him, but the rewards both now and in eternity far outweigh any temporary hardship we may be called to endure:

> Then Jesus said to his disciples, If any man would come after me, let him give up all, and take up his cross, and come after me.
>
> Because whoever has a desire to keep his life safe will have it taken from him; but whoever gives up his life because of me, will have it given back to him.
>
> (Matthew 16:24-25)

He's God, he loves you and he's worth it! Talk to him like this:

> Thank you, Jesus, for rescuing me from eternal condemnation and separation from you. Thank you for taking the punishment I should have received for all my natural

disobedience to you. I believe with all my heart that you are the living Son of God. You demonstrated your amazing love for me by suffering a cruel death on a cross. You took the punishment I deserve. The blood you shed washes me clean. I am totally forgiven and have peace with God. I surrender myself in total obedience to you. I'm beginning a new life with you as my Saviour and Lord. I want to draw closer to you each day from now on. Amen.

When television had just become commercially available the picture was only black and white. Before coloured television was invented some entrepreneur brought out a tinted filter, which would fit over your screen to produce the effect of colour. Of course, when real colour television arrived the old plastic filters were quickly assigned to the scrap heap. When I became a Christian it was like the transformation from black and white to a radiant spectrum of colour. When you hand over your life to Jesus your world lights up with all the hues of the rainbow, and you begin to see everything from a different point of view.

As you submit to God's rule over every area of your life you are gradually transformed into the person he designed you to be. This is not automatic, because you still have your free will! Every step of the way you can refuse to go forward in the direction in which God is pointing you, or you can allow him to lead you on, knowing that he cares deeply for you and wants the best for you. Each choice you make needs to be surrendered to the will of God. God's Holy Spirit will guide you as you meditate on his Word, the Bible.

> *And I say to you, Make requests, and they will be answered; what you are searching for, you will get; when you give the sign, the door will be open to you.*
>
> *For to everyone who makes a request, it will be given; and he who is searching will get his desire; and to him who gives the sign, the door will be open.*
>
> *(Luke 11:9-10)*

His Spirit is not an 'it' or an ethereal quality or substance. He is a person. If you have sincerely invited him into your life, God has taken up residence in your heart, the centre of your being. God exists in three distinct but unified personalities – the Trinity, three in one. There is God the Father, Creator of the Universe, God the Son, Jesus Christ, who became a man and God the Holy Spirit, who is the presence of God within the human heart. There is one God, but he reveals himself in three forms. Allow his Spirit to readjust your thinking. He will give you a new outlook on every aspect of life, bringing your heart in line with his purposes:

> *And let not your behaviour be like that of this world, but be changed and made new in mind, so that by experience you may have knowledge of the good and pleasing and complete purpose of God.*
>
> *(Romans 12:2)*

The Everlasting, Indestructible Kingdom

Jesus set up a new Kingdom, which is known as the Church. The founder members were the men he trained during his three-year ministry. If you try to live the Christian life in isolation, your faith will die. You are like one of a number of red hot coals in a fireplace. If you separate yourself from the other glowing embers, your flame will go out. Christians encourage and support each other in keeping faith alive and growing. The love Christians have for one another is a strong testimony of the power of God to the world at large.

You are also like a newly planted tree. Your roots are your faith in the Lord Jesus Christ. You grow as you draw strength from him. His invisible presence with you is the Holy Spirit. He will enable you to understand the Bible and show you God's character. If you remain rooted in him, you will produce spiritual fruit:

> *But the fruit of the Spirit is love, joy, peace, a quiet mind, kind acts, well-doing, faith,*
>
> *Gentle behaviour, control over desires: against such there is*

no law.

(Galatians 5: 22 & 23)

The Holy Spirit of Jesus will also give you gifts. The most common of these is the gift of tongues. This ability to speak in a strange new language of praise to God may come straightaway or later on in your Christian life. You may receive a gift of healing others. In *1 Corinthians 14:1* Paul says we should especially desire the gift of prophecy, which doesn't mean foretelling the future, but simply speaking out whatever God gives you to say.

You are a new creation. God has resurrected your dead spirit. You now have a new nature, but your old nature is still alive. These two natures are at war with each other. Feed your new nature but starve the old one.

> *Even so see yourselves as dead to sin, but living to God in Christ Jesus.*
>
> *For this cause do not let sin be ruling in your body which is under the power of death, so that you give way to its desires;*
>
> *(Romans 6:11-12)*
>
> *That you are to put away, in relation to your earlier way of life, the old man, which has become evil by love of deceit;*
>
> *And be made new in the spirit of your mind,*
>
> *And put on the new man, to which God has given life, in righteousness and a true and holy way of living.*
>
> *(Ephesians 4:22-24)*

As well as fighting against your old nature you also have another enemy. His name is Satan or the Devil. He used to be one of God's chief angels, but he rebelled and was banished from Heaven. God allows him temporarily to live on Earth, where he and other rebellious angelic beings bring confusion, temptation and trouble into the lives of mankind. God has provided Christians with spiritual protection against Satan's onslaught. Don't underestimate your enemy. You will need every part of the heavenly armour God has prepared for you:

> *For this reason take up all the arms of God, so that you may be able to be strong in the evil day, and, having done all, to keep your place.*
>
> *Take your place, then, having your body clothed with the true word, and having put on the breastplate of righteousness;*
>
> *Be ready with the good news of peace as shoes on your feet;*
>
> *And most of all, using faith as a cover to keep off all the flaming arrows of the Evil One.*
>
> *And take salvation for your head-dress and the sword of the Spirit, which is the word of God:*
>
> *(Ephesians 6:13-17)*

When you fail – as we all do – don't despair or give up. He understands your human weakness, and is always eager to forgive you and help you make a fresh start:

> *If we say openly that we have done wrong, he is upright and true to his word, giving us forgiveness of sins and making us clean from all evil.*
>
> *(1 John 1:9)*

God has a unique plan and purpose for you personally. You need to ask him to reveal it to you and seek his guidance and power to fulfil it.

> *For I am conscious of my thoughts about you, says the Lord, thoughts of peace and not of evil, to give you hope at the end.*
>
> *And you will go on crying to me and making prayer to me, and I will give ear to you.*
>
> *And you will be searching for me and I will be there, when you have gone after me with all your heart.*
>
> *(Jeremiah 29:11-13)*

We shall all be called to account for how we spent our lives:

> *For we all have to come before Christ to be judged; so that every one of us may get his reward for the things done in the*

body, good or bad.

(2 Corinthians 5:10)

God promises us many good things, if we continue to serve him faithfully. He provides for our future and keeps us protected from evil. His shield of safety will remain over us as long as we stay connected with him, but if we stray out of communication with him and go our own way, we remove ourselves from his protection. Don't get arrogant and imagine you cannot get yourself into trouble. Greater men and women than you have fallen. Even King David had a moral lapse with Bathsheba, and although he repented and received forgiveness, that episode negatively impacted the rest of his life. Temptations will come to prove your love and faithfulness, and with these you always have a choice. The good news is that God will never test you beyond your ability to resist. Giving in leads to spiritual death, so always choose life!

Whenever you have to put up with ridicule or persecution because of what you believe, do not abandon your faith. Many Christians before you have had to endure terrible suffering and even death for the sake of Jesus Christ. Right now God is bringing in his final glorious harvest, but the Bible warns that in the years just before Jesus returns to Earth there will be a short time of severe persecution for Christians, and he is coming soon. We are living in the Last Days. Be ready for Christ's return. Your reward is waiting for you in Heaven when Jesus welcomes you as one of his faithful followers:

> *His lord said to him, Well done, good and true servant: you have been true in a small thing, I will give you control over great things: take your part in the joy of your lord.*
>
> *(Matthew 25:23)*

RIGHT AND WRONG

Direction

Many modern products like cameras and audio players rely on digital technology. The basis of this is a series of *either/or* choices coded as ones or zeros (110001001110 etc.). Life itself is a series of *yes* or *no* choices, and the direction in which you jump depends on what you actually believe. God designed you, so he has provided manufacturer's instructions. The Bible is God's Manual for Successful Living, offering specific guidance on everything. If you have become a Christian by inviting Jesus Christ, God's Son, into your life, you also have God's Holy Spirit as an invisible Counsellor always available to keep you on course. He interprets and applies God's Word to your personal situation in every detail of your daily existence.

If we believe modern Freudian psychiatrists, guilt is a mere figment of the imagination to be ignored or discounted. The Bible takes the opposite view. Guilt is the intensely disturbing feeling that alerts us when we have wronged someone or offended God.

> *For my crimes have gone over my head; they are like a great weight which is more than my strength.*
>
> (Psalm 38:4)

Because God created us in his image, we have an inbuilt awareness of right and wrong. Guilt is the feeling we get when we do something that offends our conscience. Guilt can only be removed by repentance and restitution – being sincerely sorry and doing the best we can to put right what we did wrong. This brings peace, forgiveness and restoration of broken relationships. Repeatedly ignoring guilt desensitises our conscience and makes it increasingly harder for us to relate well to people or God. After committing adultery with Bathsheba and then arranging her husband's death in battle King David was bowled over with recrimination. Acknowledging his guilt, he composed this psalm to express his deep repentance and desire for reconciliation with the Lord:

> *To the chief music-maker. A Psalm. Of David. When Nathan the prophet came to him, after he had gone in to Bath-sheba. Have pity on me, O God, in your mercy; out of a full heart, take away my sin.*
>
> *Let all my wrongdoing be washed away, and make me clean from evil.*
>
> *For I am conscious of my error; my sin is ever before me.*
>
> *Make a clean heart in me, O God; give me a right spirit again.*
>
> *Do not put me away from before you, or take your holy spirit from me.*
>
> *(Psalm 51:1-3, 10-11)*

Those who deny God's existence and choose instead to believe everything came into being by chance undermine fundamental morality. There were divine laws set in place long before human rules were formulated. Humanists prefer to think truth is relative and fluid rather than absolute, but they, along with everybody else, will one day face judgement for their words and actions:

> *For you are not a God who takes pleasure in wrongdoing; there is no evil with you.*
>
> *The sons of pride have no place before you; you are a hater of all workers of evil.*
>
> *(Psalm 5:4-5)*

Never give in to the temptation to go with the crowd – 'It's okay, because everybody else does it.' Do not judge morality by comparing yourself with what other friends, neighbours or work colleagues are doing. Examine and test every action and decision by God's standards. Walk his way. Jesus said the majority were heading in the wrong direction:

> *Go in by the narrow door; for wide is the door and open is the way which goes to destruction, and great numbers go in by*

it.

> *For narrow is the door and hard the road to life, and only a small number make discovery of it.*
>
> *(Matthew 7:13-14)*

You have started off in the right direction, so don't lose the way and wander off to 'destruction.' Stay on course and at the end of the road you will find 'LIFE.'

The idea that morality is flexible and that 'rules are there to be broken' is causing havoc and chaos. Family life and values are in turmoil. A new generation is growing up with confused standards, and society in general seems unaware that God is watching:

> *The eyes of the Lord are in every place, keeping watch on the evil and the good.*
>
> *(Proverbs 15:3)*
>
> *For the eyes of the Lord are on the upright, and his ears are open to their prayers: but the face of the Lord is against those who do evil.*
>
> *(1 Peter 3:12)*

God witnesses every good and evil thing you do, speak or think. He has a heavenly video camera. Imagine if all your awful deeds from the past were replayed on a giant screen for everybody to watch. You would cringe with guilt and shame. Those who do wrong in secret and think they have got away with it will be shocked when God brings their unconfessed and unforgiven past offences out into the open:

> *But nothing is covered up, which will not come to light, or secret, which will not be made clear.*
>
> *So, whatever you have said in the dark, will come to men's hearing in the light, and what you have said secretly inside the house, will be made public from the house-tops.*
>
> *(Luke 12:2-3)*

Ten Commandments

You shall not murder. You shall not commit adultery. You shall not steal. You shall not give false testimony against your neighbour. (Exodus 20:13-16)

The Ten Commandments were given to Moses by God to provide a basic code of morality. Jesus raised the moral requirements to a higher level when he identified anger as the basic sin behind murder. His point was that a person guilty of anger was just as culpable as someone who had actually committed murder:

> *You have knowledge that it was said in old times, You may not put to death; and, Whoever puts to death will be in danger of being judged:*
>
> *But I say to you that everyone who is angry with his brother will be in danger of being judged; and he who says to his brother, Raca, will be in danger from the Sanhedrin; and whoever says, You foolish one, will be in danger of the hell of fire.*
>
> (Matthew 5:21-22)

Likewise he revealed lust as the sin behind adultery:

> *You have knowledge that it was said, You may not have connection with another man's wife:*
>
> *But I say to you that everyone whose eyes are turned on a woman with desire has had connection with her in his heart.*
>
> *And if your right eye is a cause of trouble to you, take it out and put it away from you; because it is better to undergo the loss of one part, than for all your body to go into hell.*
>
> (Matthew 5:27-29)

The tenth commandment warns against covetousness. This is not an action but a state of mind, which will give rise to other offences if indulged:

> *Let not your desire be turned to your neighbour's house, or*

> his wife or his man-servant or his woman-servant or his ox or his ass or anything which is his.
>
> (Exodus 20:17)

Jesus introduced much of his teaching with 'I tell you the truth.' He even declared himself to be 'true.' No wonder falsehood is anathema to him:

> Jesus said to him, I am the true and living way: no one comes to the Father but by me.
>
> (John 14:6)

Lying destroys trust and quickly destroys a good reputation. The fable of the shepherd boy who cried 'Wolf!' just for a joke illustrates this well. When the wolf finally did come not one soul came to the boy's rescue, so the sheep were ravaged. You can never depend on a person who is a habitual liar:

> You will send destruction on those whose words are false; the cruel man and the man of deceit are hated by the Lord.
>
> (Psalm 5:6)

People will grow to rely on your word, if you speak the simple truth consistently. Only those who are in the habit of being untruthful need to reinforce their statements by swearing by this or that to make you believe them:

> But let your words be simply, Yes or No: and whatever is more than these is of the Evil One.
>
> (Matthew 5:37)

If you want to be sure of keeping all the Ten Commandments, you just need to demonstrate love to God and to everyone you contact:

> And this, Do not be untrue in married life, Do not put to death, Do not take what is another's, Do not have desire for what is another's, and if there is any other order, it is covered by this word, Have love for your neighbour as for yourself.
>
> Love does no wrong to his neighbour, so love makes the law

complete.
(Romans 13:9-10)

Judgment

Many wicked people past and present seem to get away with murder. They escape the long arm of the law. Conversely the innocent victims of these rogues suffer lifetimes of pain and deprivation. Where is the justice? This is a recurrent theme in the Psalms:

Be lifted up, O judge of the earth; let their reward come to the men of pride.

How long will sinners, O Lord, how long will sinners have joy over us?

Words of pride come from their lips; all the workers of evil say great things of themselves.

Your people are crushed by them, O Lord, your heritage is troubled,

They put to death the widow and the guest, they take the lives of children who have no father;

And they say, Jah will not see it, the God of Jacob will not give thought to it.

(Psalm 94:2-7)

God has given man autonomy and free will. We are not programmed robots. God longs for our loving obedience, but there has to be a genuine option either to love or to hate. For God this involves a strong element of risk and patience. He has to hold back and allow us to make our choices and our mistakes. Nevertheless there have been significant occasions when he has intervened in human affairs to administer judgment and justice when he has determined the balance needed redressing. One such time was when he rescued Israel from the clutches of a cruel Pharaoh:

> On the fifteenth day of the first month they went out from Rameses; on the day after the Passover the children of Israel went out by the power of the Lord before the eyes of all the Egyptians,
>
> While the Egyptians were placing in the earth the bodies of their sons on whom the Lord had sent destruction: and their gods had been judged by him.
>
> (Numbers 33:3-4)

Another was the Flood, which drowned all but eight of the human race. Generally God exercises a very unobtrusive control, but he does promise ultimate justice – both reward and punishment:

> But by your hard and unchanged heart you are storing up wrath for yourself in the day of the revelation of God's judging in righteousness;
>
> Who will give to every man his right reward:
>
> To those who go on with good works in the hope of glory and honour and salvation from death, he will give eternal life:
>
> But to those who, from a love of competition, are not guided by what is true, will come the heat of his wrath,
>
> Trouble and sorrow on all whose works are evil, to the Jew first and then to the Greek;
>
> (Romans 2:5-9)

Jesus reminds us that God hears and judges every conversation:

> And I say to you that in the day when they are judged, men will have to give an account of every foolish word they have said.
>
> (Matthew 12:36)

The Apostle Paul warns that we will face God on Judgment Day:

> But you, why do you make yourself your brother's judge? or again, why have you no respect for your brother? because we will all have to take our place before God as our judge.

> *For it is said in the holy Writings, By my life, says the Lord, to me every knee will be bent, and every tongue will give worship to God.*
>
> *So every one of us will have to give an account of himself to God.*
>
> *(Romans 14:10-12)*

The Apostle Peter emphasises God's patience in delaying Judgment to allow time for us to turn to him, and graphically describes that future Day for the righting of wrongs, comparing it in severity with the Flood:

> *And that the world which then was came to an end through the overflowing of the waters.*
>
> *But the present heaven and the present earth have been kept for destruction by fire, which is waiting for them on the day of the judging and destruction of evil men.*
>
> *But, my loved ones, keep in mind this one thing, that with the Lord one day is the same as a thousand years, and a thousand years are no more than one day.*
>
> *The Lord is not slow in keeping his word, as he seems to some, but he is waiting in mercy for you, not desiring the destruction of any, but that all may be turned from their evil ways.*
>
> *Seeing then that all these things are coming to such an end, what sort of persons is it right for you to be, in all holy behaviour and righteousness,*
>
> *Looking for and truly desiring the coming of the day of God, when the heavens will come to an end through fire, and the substance of the earth will be changed by the great heat?*
>
> *(2 Peter 3:6-9, 11-12)*

LIFE

In God's Hands

From the moment of conception the foetus is a human being infused with life from God. Amazingly he knew all about you even before that:

> *My flesh was made by you, and my parts joined together in my mother's body.*
>
> *I will give you praise, for I am strangely and delicately formed; your works are great wonders, and of this my soul is fully conscious.*
>
> *My frame was not unseen by you when I was made secretly, and strangely formed in the lowest parts of the earth.*
>
> *Your eyes saw my unformed substance; in your book all my days were recorded, even those which were purposed before they had come into being.*
>
> *(Psalm 139:13-16)*

'Getting rid' of that precious soul before it comes to birth is not just a denial of human rights; it is murder in God's eyes:

> *And anyone who takes another's life is certainly to be put to death.*
>
> *(Leviticus 24:17)*

From the moment you were conceived God had his hand on your life. God champions the cause of the weak, and there can be no weaker stage in the life of a human being than that of a newly-conceived foetus.

> *Be not tricked; God is not made sport of: for whatever seed a man puts in, that will he get back as grain.*
>
> *Because he who puts in the seed of the flesh will of the flesh get the reward of death; but he who puts in the seed of the Spirit will of the Spirit get the reward of eternal life.*

> (Galatians 6:7-8)

At the other end of the spectrum, euthanasia is not an option. Human life is precious. God began it and it is his prerogative to end it, not ours. King David acknowledged God's sovereignty over his life:

> The chances of my life are in your hand; take me out of the hands of my haters, and of those who go after me.
>
> (Psalm 31:15)

God is the only one with the power to give you a long life. The manner and timing of a person's death should be left in his control:

> The fear of the Lord gives long life, but the years of the evil-doer will be cut short.
>
> (Proverbs 10:27)

Taking human life is forbidden, whether it is somebody else's or your own. Leave that decision to the one who knows best:

> A Polish man, in a coma for nineteen years, recently returned to consciousness and began relearning how to live. Doctors had advised Jan's wife, Gertruda that he would not live, but she never gave up hope. 'Now he can sit in his wheelchair and we have breakfast and coffee together,' she said. Gertruda added, 'I would fly into a rage every time someone would say that people like him should be euthanized, so they don't suffer. I believed Janek would recover, this is my great reward for all the care, faith and love.' In response Jan was quoted as saying, 'It was Gertruda that saved me and I will never forget it.' (Source: Associated Press; February 2008)

Poverty

What Darwin failed to grasp with his *Survival of the Fittest* doctrine is that God is actually a supporter of the underdog. He looks out for the weak and helpless and encourages his followers to do the same:

> *For there will never be a time when there are no poor in the land; and so I give orders to you, Let your hand be open to your countrymen, to those who are poor and in need in your land.*
>
> *(Deuteronomy 15:11)*

People often make remarks like, 'If there was a god, he would not allow that to happen.' What they do not appreciate is that God is even more moved than they are by the plight of the world's downtrodden individuals:

> *Who gives their rights to those who are crushed down; and gives food to those who are in need of it: the Lord makes the prisoners free;*
>
> *The Lord makes open the eyes of the blind; the Lord is the lifter up of those who are bent down; the Lord is a lover of the upright;*
>
> *The Lord takes care of those who are in a strange land; he gives help to the widow and to the child who has no father; but he sends destruction on the way of sinners.*
>
> *(Psalm 146:7-9)*

God is well aware of every victim of injustice, avarice and apathy, but he strongly desires us to feel the same concern:

> *And God said, Truly, I have seen the grief of my people in Egypt, and their cry because of their cruel masters has come to my ears; for I have knowledge of their sorrows;*
>
> *(Exodus 3:7)*

God's response to his people's wretched existence under the oppressive Pharaoh working them to death in Egypt was to intervene by equipping Moses to head up his rescue operation. A series of increasingly devastating plagues announced by Moses and instigated by God finally drove Pharaoh to release his Hebrew slaves. God acted compassionately and decisively and he expects us to do the same:

> *The religion which is holy and free from evil in the eyes of our God and Father is this: to take care of children who have no fathers and of widows who are in trouble, and to keep oneself untouched by the world.*
>
> *(James 1:27)*

Marriage

God's plan for the continuation of the human race from the very beginning was that children should be born into a loving family, where a mother and father are committed to each other for life. He designed sexual relations to create a unique bond between the husband and wife:

> *For this cause will a man go away from his father and his mother and be joined to his wife; and they will be one flesh.*
>
> *(Genesis 2:24)*

Children need to develop in a secure, loving environment with boundaries in place. God instituted the sacrament of marriage to nurture and encourage the eternal love and commitment of both partners:

> *Let married life be honoured among all of you and not made unclean; for men untrue in married life will be judged by God.*
>
> *(Hebrews 13:4)*

Promiscuity destroys long-term family stability for momentary pleasure. Loose sexual morality is a blatant feature of modern times. It is prevalent all around the globe and is encouraged by certain television shows and the media in general. These times are prophesied by the Apostle Paul in his letter to Timothy, where he refers to them as 'the Last Days.' Things are already spiralling out of control and heading for God's final Judgment:

> *But be certain of this, that in the last days times of trouble will come.*
>
> *For men will be lovers of self, lovers of money, uplifted in pride, given to bitter words, going against the authority of their fathers, never giving praise, having no religion,*
>
> *Without natural love, bitter haters, saying evil of others, violent and uncontrolled, hating all good,*
>
> *False to their friends, acting without thought, lifted up in mind, loving pleasure more than God;*
>
> *(2 Timothy 3:1-4)*

The current lobbying for same-sex marriage has no foundation in the Bible. The scriptural focus of marriage is the child's long-term welfare. If governments allow children to be adopted and brought up by two 'fathers' or two 'mothers,' we are on a slippery slope. If two 'fathers' are permitted, why not have three or four or none? History is littered with civilizations which have disintegrated because of a downward spiral of immorality, wreaking havoc with the family unit.

Marriage by definition is a natural union producing offspring. Redefining the unnatural union of same sex partners as "marriage" automatically bestows the expectation of the right to foster children, whether or not the men or women are suitably motivated and gifted. Children conceived from a male + female union need to be cared for by a mother + father. Nature demands that the offspring have a basic human right to be cared for by both parents. Children deprived of a mother, father or both suffer the consequences long-term.

Same-sex "marriage" produces no progeny, so its ultimate logical conclusion is extinction. If this redefinition becomes law, those seeking to undermine the family as the basic unit of society will have won a key battle, which will rapidly destroy the fabric of civilisation. There is no need for same-sex marriage, because these couples can receive all the legal benefits provided for married couples by entering a civil partnership.

Physical Wellbeing

The success of television shows where obese men and women compete to achieve the biggest weight loss is a testimony to the out of control eating habits of a significant percentage of our population. In spite of intensive publicity about their harmful effects, the craving for drugs is an escalating cause of misery to modern society, especially the rich and famous and the younger generation. Even some Christians experience hardship in overcoming their addiction to tobacco, but with God's help they do. The Bible does not prohibit the drinking of alcohol, but only doing it to excess. Your body was designed by God and is described in the following verses as a 'temple,' because God wants to reside there. This should warn you not to desecrate your body with harmful drugs or excessive food and alcohol:

> *Or are you not conscious that your body is a house for the Holy Spirit which is in you, and which has been given to you by God? and you are not the owners of yourselves;*
>
> *For a payment has been made for you: let God be honoured in your body.*
>
> *(1 Corinthians 6:19-20)*

Your body is the dwelling place for the Holy Spirit, so do not pollute that temple with harmful substances:

> *Do you not see that you are God's holy house, and that the Spirit of God has his place in you?*
>
> *If anyone makes the house of God unclean, God will put an end to him; for the house of God is holy, and you are his house.*
>
> *(1 Corinthians 3:16-17)*

The consumption of wine is not condemned, but drunkenness is, yet these days getting drunk seems to be the main objective and the measure of a party's success. Swilling down beer, lager, wine and spirits is an expected ingredient at many social events.

> *And do not take overmuch wine by which one may be overcome, but be full of the Spirit;*
>
> *(Ephesians 5:18)*

There are a number of clear warnings in the Bible that those who habitually overeat or repeatedly drink themselves into a stupor will end up on the poverty level:

> *Do not be among those who give themselves to wine-drinking, or among those who make themselves full with meat:*
>
> *For those who take delight in drink and feasting will come to be in need; and through love of sleep a man will be poorly clothed.*
>
> *(Proverbs 23:20-21)*

Those who have overcome these cravings with God's help testify that he gave them the strength and determination to conquer their excesses. The first step is admitting that you have a problem, and then you can trust him to get you back on track.

When the world was young, fruit and vegetables provided all the nourishment people needed:

> *And out of the earth the Lord made every tree to come, delighting the eye and good for food; and in the middle of the garden, the tree of life and the tree of the knowledge of good and evil.*
>
> *(Genesis 2:9)*

Meat was off the menu, because alternative nutrition was readily available:

> *Thorns and waste plants will come up, and the plants of the field will be your food;*

(Genesis 3:18)

Due to the dramatically changed environment after the Flood God modified the vegetarian aspect of the curse on Adam to permit the addition of meat to man's diet:

> *And the fear of you will be strong in every beast of the earth and every bird of the air; everything which goes on the land, and all the fishes of the sea, are given into your hands.*
>
> *Every living and moving thing will be food for you; I give them all to you as before I gave you all green things.*
>
> *(Genesis 9:2-3)*

Having said that, there may be occasions when a purely vegetable diet is healthier. In Babylon Daniel and his friends refused the rich food and wine provided by the king and requested vegetables instead. After only ten days they were noticeably healthier looking than their companions (Daniel 1:8-16).

Sex

God loves you whether you are currently heterosexual or homosexual, and Jesus poured out his life-blood to bring you forgiveness. We have no right to outcast or condemn any other human being, because not one of us measures up to God's standard of perfection. In varying degrees we are all 'sick' and 'sinners.'

> *And Jesus, answering, said to them, Those who are well have no need of a medical man, but those who are ill.*
>
> *I have come, not to get the upright, but sinners, so that they may be turned from their sins.*
>
> *(Luke 5:31-32)*

However, God's blueprint for sexual partnership is male with female. This is the way he set it up, and with his help you can readjust in harmony with his design. If the successful continuation of the human race depended on just men or just women, God would have designed our physiology in a totally different manner. The first two people were Adam and Eve, not Adam and Steve. Male and female are complementary, not interchangeable. The natural world flourishes on the male plus female arrangement. Children need the balance of a mum and a dad influencing their lives for healthy development. God's word has a lot to say about how husbands are to love their wives and how wives should relate to their husbands, but it condemns homosexuality and warns of severe judgment to come:

> *But before they had gone to bed, the men of the town, all the men of Sodom, came round the house, young and old, from every part of the town;*
>
> *And crying out to Lot, they said, Where are the men who came to your house this night? Send them out to us, so that we may take our pleasure with them.*
>
> *Then the Lord sent fire and flaming smoke raining down from heaven on Sodom and Gomorrah.*
>
> *(Genesis 19:4-5 & 24)*

Homosexual and lesbian relationships are described as unnatural and perverse. The penalty for such perversion comes in the form of sexually transmitted diseases including gonorrhoea, syphilis and AIDS, which sadly can be passed on accidentally to heterosexuals (through contaminated blood transfusions, for example):

> *For this reason God gave them up to evil passions, and their women were changing the natural use into one which is unnatural:*
>
> *And in the same way the men gave up the natural use of the woman and were burning in their desire for one another, men doing shame with men, and getting in their bodies the right reward of their evil-doing.*
>
> *(Romans 1:26-27)*

Michael Glatze was founding editor of Young Gay America magazine, but has had a radical transformation that has brought him out of that lifestyle:

> *Homosexuality came easy to me, because I was already weak. My mom died when I was 19. My father had died when I was 13. At an early age, I was already confused about who I was and how I felt about others. My confusion about 'desire' and the fact that I noticed I was 'attracted' to guys made me put myself into the 'gay' category at age 14. It took me almost 16 years to discover that homosexuality itself is not exactly 'virtuous.' It was difficult for me to clarify my feelings on the issue, given that my life was so caught up in it. Homosexuality, delivered to young minds, is by its very nature pornographic. It destroys impressionable minds and confuses their developing sexuality; I did not realize this, however, until I was 30 years old. I was asked to speak at the prestigious Harvard's Kennedy School of Government in 2005. It was, after viewing my words on a videotape of that 'performance,' that I began to seriously doubt what I was doing with my life and influence. Knowing no one who I could approach with my questions and my doubts, I turned to God; I'd developed a growing relationship with God, thanks to a debilitating bout with intestinal cramps caused by the upset stomach-inducing behaviours I'd been engaged in. Homosexuality prevents us from finding our true self within. We cannot see the truth when we're blinded by homosexuality. Every time I was tempted to lust, I noticed it, caught it, dealt with it. I called it what it was, and then just let it disappear on its own. In my experience, 'coming out' from under the influence of the homosexual mind-set was the most liberating, beautiful and astonishing thing I've ever experienced in my entire life. [WorldNetDaily; March 2008]*

God's purpose for our lives is to provide us with the motivation and spiritual power to be transformed gradually into people who spend our lives giving priority to his requirements and directions.

> *Now the works of the flesh are clear, which are these: evil*

> *desire, unclean things, wrong use of the senses,*
>
> *Envy, uncontrolled drinking and feasting, and such things: of which I give you word clearly, even as I did in the past, that they who do such things will have no part in the kingdom of God.*
>
> *(Galatians 5:19 & 21)*

Indulgence in sexual perversion will deprive you of your heavenly destination! Men in particular need to avoid giving in to this temptation. It is not only wrong in itself, but it can breed lustful desires, resulting in crimes of rape often associated with murder. It is also responsible for the multiplication of brothels in the guise of massage parlours, rampant prostitution and the growth of the abominable child sex racket. How do you fight this satanic evil? The antidote for impure thoughts is meditation on things that are wholesome and positive:

> *For the rest, my brothers, whatever things are true, whatever things have honour, whatever things are upright, whatever things are holy, whatever things are beautiful, whatever things are of value, if there is any virtue and if there is any praise, give thought to these things.*
>
> *(Philippians 4:8)*

The word of God is powerfully effective in achieving its goals.

This is just an introduction to what is to some a huge issue. For an in-depth treatment I recommend a scholarly, but also very practical and down-to-earth paperback entitled 'God Sex' by Dr. Jillian Sweetman. She offers valuable material on every aspect of this sensitive subject with contributions covering numerous personal points of view.

Conservation

The Theory of Evolution maintains that an upward progression from simple to complex is going on, but the 2nd Law of Thermodynamics suggests otherwise:

> *In any cyclic process the entropy (a measure of the disorder of a system) will either increase or remain the same. [18th July 2008; hyperphysics.phy-astr.gsu.edu/hbase/thermo/seclaw.html]*

In simple terms this means that the Universe is gradually deteriorating. Global warming, the breaking up of the ozone layer, the melting of the Polar ice caps, increase in earthquake activity, growing pollution, drought, famine, proliferation of viruses, cancer, epidemics and plagues strongly indicate that life on our planet is worsening. The Bible has an explanation as to why this is happening. God created everything perfectly in the beginning, and all the delights of that beautiful world were there for Adam and Eve to enjoy, including a close friendship with their Creator. God wanted their love, but for this to be genuine he had to allow them the option of disobedience. He specified just one fruit that they were not to touch or the result would be death. After Adam and Eve rebelled against his authority God had to inflict on them the judgment he had decreed. Death – not immediate, but gradual – entered the world. Along with this came other changes as God pronounced a series of curses, by which is meant the verbalising of the negative effects resulting from this act of disobedience. First he addressed Satan:

> *'And there will be war between you and the woman and between your seed and her seed: by him will your head be crushed and by you his foot will be wounded. (Genesis 3:15)*

God here was speaking to the serpent, the Devil and prophesying that he would continue inflicting harm on humanity, but that one of the woman's offspring – Jesus – would 'crush his head,' that is, defeat him. Jesus achieved this by his death and resurrection. Satan is our beaten enemy. Having expressed this curse on Satan, God spoke next to Eve:

> *To the woman he said, Great will be your pain in childbirth; in sorrow will your children come to birth; still your desire will be for your husband, but he will be your master.*
>
> *(Genesis 3:16)*

Having children was never intended to be such a painful experience. Also male and female equality was lost at this point. Down through history man has dominated woman. This balance is only restored through faith in Jesus Christ:

> *There is no Jew or Greek, servant or free, male or female: because you are all one in Jesus Christ.*
>
> *(Galatians 3:28)*

For the pronouncement of the final curse God turned to the man:

> *And to Adam he said, Because you gave ear to the voice of your wife and took of the fruit of the tree which I said you were not to take, the earth is cursed on your account; in pain you will get your food from it all your life.*
>
> *Thorns and waste plants will come up, and the plants of the field will be your food;*
>
> *With the hard work of your hands you will get your bread till you go back to the earth from which you were taken: for dust you are and to the dust you will go back.*
>
> *(Genesis 3:17-19)*

Every gardener and farmer knows the backbreaking curse of weeds, but the burden of working hard to make a living is universal, and so is the ultimate return to dust. Although not all the effects of Adam and Eve's disobedience are spelt out in detail in the Genesis curses, many other things evident today bear out the following:

> *For every living thing was put under the power of change, not by its desire, but by him who made it so, in hope*

> *That all living things will be made free from the power of death and will have a part with the free children of God in glory.*
>
> *For we are conscious that all living things are weeping and sorrowing in pain together till now.*
>
> *(Romans 8:20-22)*

A school colleague of mine had been made responsible for environmental issues. As the mail arrived it was sorted according to subject headings and assigned to pigeon-holes for teachers with special oversight of specific areas of responsibility. One morning the secretary breezed into the staff room brandishing a large, brown package and was greeted with howls of laughter when she asked, 'Who's the teacher in charge of Saving the Planet?'

> *And the Lord God took the man and put him in the garden of Eden to do work in it and take care of it.*
>
> *(Genesis 2:15)*

Certainly we should do all in our power to look after the beautiful world God has created, but the indisputable fact is that it is wearing out, and its resources are running down as the world population grows astronomically.

Green issues are important, but there are weightier matters deserving our attention. Hold on lightly to what is temporal, and firmly grasp whatever relates to eternity. While doing the best we can to hand over an environmentally healthy earth to our descendants, we need to remember that sometime in the future God is going to recycle the whole Universe:

> *And I saw a new heaven and a new earth: for the first heaven and the first earth were gone; and there was no more sea.*
>
> *(Revelation 21:1)*

This is good news for those trusting in God through his Son Jesus Christ.

But the present heaven and the present earth have been kept for destruction by fire, which is waiting for them on the day of the judging and destruction of evil men.

But, my loved ones, keep in mind this one thing, that with the Lord one day is the same as a thousand years, and a thousand years are no more than one day.

The Lord is not slow in keeping his word, as he seems to some, but he is waiting in mercy for you, not desiring the destruction of any, but that all may be turned from their evil ways.

But the day of the Lord will come like a thief; and in that day the heavens will be rolled up with a great noise, and the substance of the earth will be changed by violent heat, and the world and everything in it will be burned up.

Seeing then that all these things are coming to such an end, what sort of persons is it right for you to be, in all holy behaviour and righteousness,

Looking for and truly desiring the coming of the day of God, when the heavens will come to an end through fire, and the substance of the earth will be changed by the great heat?

But having faith in his word, we are looking for a new heaven and a new earth, which will be the resting-place of righteousness.

(2 Peter 3:7-13)

The old worn-out Universe is to be replaced by a new model, where we shall be able to live in peace and harmony with God and our fellow man with nothing evil to wreck it!

<><><><><>

Printed in Great Britain
by Amazon.co.uk, Ltd.,
Marston Gate.